CLEAR
THE INSIGHT
OF
YOUR LIFE...

Birister Sharma

Copyright © 2022 Birister Sharma

All Rights Reserved.

Dedicated to my loving wife....

Pallabi Devi Sharma

I surrendered to you, O my
Lord……

"Om Namah Shivaya"

Table of Contents

One word

In every juncture of life, there are many ups and downs. And every moment you need motivation and encouragement. It may be from yourself and from your dear ones. However, the question arises, how? If nobody is around you, then, it's only you to motivate and encourage yourself; because, life is a lone journey. First think and then act.

Always remember, that you're the only one who can change yourself and nobody can change you.

If you want to light the darkness of your life, then enlighten your vision of life and clear your mission of life....

᭫***᭫

1. Life is full of Mysteries

Life is full of mysteries.

Sometimes it shows you green trees,

Invites you with its delicious fruits,

And sometimes it gets off with its bitter fluids.

Life gives you full of surprises.

Sometimes it gives you beautiful prizes.

It shows lovely images,

And sometimes it shows you fake mirages.

In life, both happiness and sorrow

Come one after another in a row.

Life is for a moment,

Full of lament.

When it says goodbye,

When everything remains lie,

When it stops its flow,

You don't know.

What will going to happen to you?

Now, today and tomorrow,

You don't know anything.

But every moment you're heading towards its destiny.

It's the reality.

Life is always uncertain.

It's an ordinary curtain.

How many houses you've built;

How many lives you've healed;

It only counts.

Who'll go to remember you?

Who'll forget you?

It doesn't matter.

How long you spend your life in this world,

It doesn't matter.

But how you will spend your life in this world,

It does matter.

Before anything going too late,

Open your life's gate.

Do something great

So that someday, somebody remembers your name after your death.

Life is beautiful.

You can make it more beautiful.

Everything is in your hands.

What do you want in your life?

It's up to you

Whether you want to dwell in the heaven

Or in the hell.

Both Earth and Heaven, is within your reach.

It's up to you

Whether you want to relish in the garden of flowers

Or in the land of weeds.

Whether you want a sand stone

Or a gem stone.

It's in your hands.

Life is like day and night.

Every day is a new dawn and a new dusk.

Sometime life is like a fading autumn,

And sometimes it is like a blooming spring.

It's the reality of life.

You must accept it!

But you can't escape from it.

It's the law of life.

Try to taste the spirit of every season of your life,

And spread its beauty everywhere.

If you ever can't build a grand mansion.

Then what!

You can build a house of love.

If you ever can't live a life of luxury.

Then what!

You can live a life of happiness.

Love your life.

Love your fellow mates,

Give them the sweet flavor of your life.

Life is a journey of one time.

You don't know the journey of another world.

Whatever you have

Everything is right now.

So, live the life of every moment,

And make it more meaningful and beautiful.

Our journey of life,

Begins with our first breath,

Ends with our last breath.

We find our natives,

We get our relatives.

We have to leave one day,

But, nobody can't say.

Our life is a drama of uncertainties.

The end with the fall of a curtain of life.

Every moment of this life is precious for us.

Every day is a day of the bonus.

We all are travelers,

Nobody is permanent dwellers.

So, never hurt anybody.

Despite you get hurt.

Give love,

Receive love.

Life is in the midst of happiness and sorrow.

It is like day and night.

Learn to smile,

Learn to laugh.

But as long as you survive,

Always try to revive,

Because it is our journey of life.

Every moment of this life is precious for us,

Every day is a day of the bonus.

~***~

2. War

Your mind is the battlefield.

Every seed of war sprouted here.

It is between the two things,

Divine and evil,

Good and bad,

Success and failure,

Happiness and sorrow.

It is the war of your inner feelings.

It is never ending struggle.

It is your lone war.

But you've to fight.

You've to come out.

You've to regain your lost kingdom of peace.

You've to liberate yourself from this war.

Your mind is the battlefield,

Every seed of war sprouted here.

⁓***⁓

3. Your vision

What you want to be?

What you want to see?

Everything depends upon your vision.

Find out your reason.

Every event of life is matters to you,

And it asks you its demand.

You must know the right command.

Guide yourself in the wide direction

To succeed in your mission.

Know your inner potential, which is unlimited.

Don't spend your life like a timid.

Open your mind, which you keep locked,

It's time to unlock.

Wash your unclean eyes,

Wear out your old fashion,

Try to be wise.

Everything which is unseen,

Now, it is visible.

It is your time to walk

To get your golden luck.

Visualize your ideas to the world

So that you can shine like a diamond.

﹏***﹏

4. *Only you can change yourself!*

Change yourself.

Change is the universal law.

You can't change the minds of others...

You can't change the hearts of others.....

You can't change the emotions of others....

You can't change the feelings of others.....

You can't change the thoughts of others...

You can't change the dreams of others....

You can't change the ambitions of others...

You can't change the ideas of others....

You can't change the decisions of others....

You can't change the attitudes of others....

You can't change the actions of others.....

You can't change the lives of others....

You can't change the worlds of others....

However, you can change your own mind.....

You can change your own heart....

You can change your own emotions....

You can change your own feelings....

You can change your own thoughts......

You can change your own dreams....

You can change your own ambitions...

You can change your own ideas....

You can change your own decisions....

You can change your own attitudes....

You can change your own actions.....

You can change your own life....

You can change your own world....

You need change.

It's true that you can't bring hundred percent changes in your life,

At least you can bring one percent change in your life.

If you ever can't get the ocean of water,

Then what!

At least you can get a few drops of rainwater.

Nobody can change you.

Only you can change yourself.

If you ever can't get the ocean of water,

Then what!

At least you can get a few drops of rainwater.

⌢***⌣

5. A Heart of Mine

A heart of mine

In a long lifeline.

I've a lot of hope,

And a thirst of love.

Sometime, I felt a heart alone,

And living in unknown.

Hurt by a spine,

Which wounded my desire.

And set it into the fire.

But, I'm not getting tired,

Because, God blesses His stir.

He tied me in His love wire,

And I couldn't get retire,

He changed my entire human's attire.

Don't feel tire in your life, even if your desires are set in fire…..

You have to travel a thousand miles….

⸫***⸫

6. A Game

My life is like a game,

It has many names.

I was caught by the hands of dame,

And she took away my fame.

My face felt ashamed,

And my legs turned lame;

I was like her tame.

Who will get rid of me?

Only my Heaven knows!

My life lost its aim.

Your life is like a game....

Play it well....

⁓***⁓

7. Human's Life

Born as a child,

Fall in the mother's lap.

He never be alone,

Meets his fellow mates,

And bind in the native bonds.

Grown as a young,

He desires to earn.

Whatever he wished;

Tried to succeed,

Forgot his moralities,

And met miseries and sorrows.

As an old,

He thinks and realized.

His cultures and character shows

His life span.

His noble deeds

Makes him great.

His life is for a day

End with death.

In the journey of life, miseries and sorrows are natural....

Accept them and move on....

⁓***⁓

8. A Drama

Our life is a drama,

Without rehearsal.

Where you, we and I,

To act and play the role.

An actor and an actress as a whole

On the stage of earth.

Our life is a drama,

As the curtain rises, it begins.

The story, full of mysteries,

Woes and tears are the emotions.

Jokes and laughs are the fun,

Praises and criticisms are the rewards.

Our life is a drama,

The rich or the poor; the king or the beggar,

Be the characters.

But, each part got its significance.

The few get

Special appearance;

The few remains as the glittering stones,

And a few ever shines as the shining stars.

Your life is like a drama...

Play and act well....

~***~

9. Plan

It's a golden rule,

It's an old rule,

Which makes the life in control,

And makes the man in good role.

It's a routine,

Changes our lifeline.

It's a chart,

Which visualize our part.

It reflects our future,

And effects our nature.

It moves the life in order,

And makes the man in proper.

It's a plan which changes the course of life of a man.

It's a plan which changes the course of life of a man.

‿***‿

10. Longevity

It's all about uncertainties;

No one could say,

Neither foreteller nor astrologer.

It's the life,

Which is neither short nor prolong,

Neither fix nor long.

It's depending upon its own;

An unsolved puzzle.

It's the longevity of the unknown,

And makes the life dazzle.

It has initial point,

But has no final point.

It has entry door,

But has no exit door.

Some live a long life,

Some live a short life.

It's the tragedy of life.

It comes to the end at any time,

So, leave some remarkable thing.

It's the longevity of life,

So, leave some valuable thing.

Some live a long life,

Some live a short life.

It's the tragedy of life.

It comes to the end at any time,

So, leave some remarkable thing.

◟***◞

11. The Golden Rays

O Losing and weak heart!

Why you're wasting your valuable birth?

You haven't seen the sparkling gem,

How much it resists the stresses and the burning flame.

Then only it transforms into a new shape,

And all likes to have.

Why not you see the clear sky?

Open your clouded eyes to view high.

Look at the king of the air,

The Eagle, which always fly so high with dare.

Try to be like the king of the jungle

Who walks lonely, but nobody tries to mingle.

Why you're trapping yourself in self- made illusion of the net?

Set a new target.

Come out!

Stop it!

Why you're keeping nail on your own way?

Create a new horizon for your own golden ray.

Why you're trapping yourself in self- made illusion of the net?

Set a new target.

Come out!

Stop it!

‿***‿

12. Desire

It's your desire,

Like the fire.

It burns,

So, try to learn.

Whatever you did mistake,

Try to retake.

Don't be too late,

On your way to make.

It's your life.

Keep it safe.

Try to fly

As much as you can, high.

Hold your heart to fight

For your own right.

Then, you'll be the star of the sky.

You'll ever shine in the above sky.

Try to fly

As much as you can, high.

Hold your heart to fight

For your own right.

⸛***⸜

13. Mind

It's full of might,

You've to guide.

It's unique.

It reaches the highest zenith.

It is faster than the wind.

It helps to win.

It is the main centre,

Allow your heart and soul to enter.

It is the host,

Don't try to lose.

It is the power of the infinite,

Set your goal definite.

It is the source of energy; extract,

Turn your new ideas; exact.

Concentrate on the right incident,

Build your hidden confident.

You've to ignite it

In order to get your bright light in it.

Don't make it nomad,

Else, you'll become mad.

You need to direct

  To raise it erects.

It is your mind the main cause

Which you can't pause.

Only you can tame,

Then you get your fame.

Your mind is very powerful.

Control it.

Never allow it to wander anywhere....

Guide and lead it to the right direction....

⌣***⌣

14. Conscience

Lying in your heart's deep,

Nobody dares to peep.

It is always thinking,

You're at the touch of linking.

It ever modifies

To cleanse your mind and to purify.

It constantly extracts

To turn you in the form of exact.

Every time it reacts,

And tells you to act.

Your mind may cheat,

But, it honestly heed.

It stands in your way to guide

To show you the path of light.

Nobody can observe you, but its eyes judge,

And you're under watch.

Whatever may be the Condition, it grasps to control,

And it plays an important role.

It is none other than your own voice of soul,

Try to hear it and hold.

Your conscience is the voice of your soul.

Hear it...

Follow it....

⸾***⸾

15. Patience

A rope, which is tight,

Always binds you might.

It moves slowly,

But, always non-stop flow.

It doesn't allow you to be haste

And stops you from waste.

It teaches you the best lesson

Which is never ending moral of the session.

It helps you to take your decision free,

So that you can widely see.

Its taste is bitter,

But, its result makes you better.

It acts as your true friend,

One who is wholly trained.

In your every agony of trouble,

It makes you stable.

You can stand like the rock,

And nobody ever tries to stroke.

It is your patience,

It will make you priceless essence.

To keep your patience is a bitter test,

But, its result is sweet.

⤳***⤳

16. Thought

Every thought that comes to you

Always affects you.

Your inner image,

Your outer image,

All are reflected on you,

Without it, nobody can live.

Because, it's the art of living.

Whether you're right or you're wrong,

Whether you're weak or you're strong.

You're merely a medium of reaction,

But, all are guided by its action.

It becomes wild when it is not properly tame.

Your ways of life become lame.

Before, it'll get dirt and turn impure

And spoil you, make it pure.

Your thoughts become wild when they are not properly tame.

Control and tame your thoughts.

⌇***⌇

17. Attitude

Our life is all about attitude.

Lift us to the greatest altitude.

It boosts our might

And helps us to reach the topmost height.

It raises our inner power of will

And make us like the giant hill.

Flows the energy of charm

And hold our weak arm.

Our heart never falls

And there are no doubts of call.

We could see the lightning in the darkness

And our life starts dancing in the brightness.

Our life becomes bold and tall head

And we ever ready to march ahead.

Your attitude lifts you to the greatest altitude.

It boosts your might, and helps you to reach the topmost height.

⌇***⌇

18. Luck

Your destiny is long,

So, tune your heroic song.

It is full of sharp nails,

Ever stand to fail.

But, you've nothing to mourn,

Sound your alarm horn.

Whatever your peer says,

Wherever they direct your ways,

And whatever you've seen,

Forget it and keep your keen.

Keep your eyes in the right act,

And try to search your tact.

If your steps are slow,

There is nothing to blow.

Don't worry!

Don't feel sorry!

Hold your vibrating nerve

And control your cravings.

If you ever fail to bounce,

But, never give up pouncing.

When you begin your walk,

You'll surely get your luck.

When you begin your walk,

You'll surely get your luck.

⌣***⌣

19. Respect

Whoever he is?

Whoever she is?

Open your heart to respect,

And keep you expect.

It is the warmest gratitude,

Express your attitude.

Whether senior

Or junior.

As you greet,

As you get treated.

It is your manner

Which tells about you, what you've learnt from your elder.

If your head is bowed,

You don't become low.

But, your happiness adds,

And you'll feel glad.

We're civilize man,

We're not savage.

Even the beast knows,

How to show?

If your parents are old,

Then they are your valuable gold.

Don't feel shame,

You should respect them.

Pay your homage,

To brighten their image,

It is your merit

Which you inherit,

Because when you earn,

Then only you can return.

When you follow,

You become a good fellow.

It turns you great,

And you get your real mate.

Open your heart to respect,

And keep you expect.

It is the warmest gratitude,

Express your attitude.

⁓***⁓

20. Wicket Habit

In the beginning, it is very sweet,

Later it'll start haunting you and it'll become difficult to quit.

It binds you with the fencing of string,

And you will trap in its hanging link.

Once you'll involve,

You'll totally dissolve.

You'll become heavy,

And your life will flow in waves.

Your pious life will adulterate,

Your thoughts will slowly penetrate.

It'll tie you in its dark cave,

And you will not move your pave.

It is like the deep ditch

Where you'll ever meet hitch.

If you'll become its slave,

You'll get hard slap.

It is like a gum

Makes your mind dumb.

Everything will go to stick,

And nothing will come in your pick.

It will form like a thick layer,

And every time it'll wear.

It is like the water with oil,

Your purity will spoil.

It'll weaken your ability,

And ruin your quality.

So, don't swim in the shallow sea!

Don't spend like the life of the hollow tree.

Take a close look,

In order to catch it with your hook.

***In the beginning, the wicked habit is very
sweet,***

***Later it'll start haunting you and it'll
become very difficult to quit.***

‿***‿

21. Everything is not for you

Everything that comes in your mind

Is not always suitable for you.

Don't feel sorry and worry!

Keep your hopes alive!

Everything that you feel in your heart

Is not always pleasant for you.

Don't feel sorry and worry!

Keep your hopes alive!

Everything that you see with your eyes

Is not always visible for you.

Don't feel sorry and worry!

Keep your hopes alive!

Everything that you hear with your ears

Is not always true for you.

Don't feel sorry and worry!

Keep your hopes alive!

Everything that you smell with your nose

Is not always sweet for you.

Don't feel sorry and worry!

Keep your hopes alive!

Everything that you taste with your tongue

Is not always delicious for you.

Don't feel sorry and worry!

Keep your hopes alive!

Everything that you speak with your mouth

Is not always correct for you.

Don't feel sorry and worry!

Keep your hopes alive!

Everything that you smile with your lips

Is not always enjoyable for you.

Don't feel sorry and worry!

Keep your hopes alive!

Everything that you touch with your hands

Is not always tender for you.

Don't feel sorry and worry!

Keep your hopes alive!

Everything that you desire in life

Is not for you.

Don't feel sorry and worry!

Keep your hopes alive!

Everything that you desire in life is not for you.

Don't feel sorry and worry!

Keep your hopes alive!

⁓***⁓

22. *Anger*

It is the anger,

Very dangerous.

It is like a burning fire,

Gives you a sweating tire,

It burns your heart,

It burns your art.

It is very hot,

Burn you a lot.

So, never try to ignite,

Because you'll get bitten, whenever you invite.

It is an inflammable flame,

Its flying ashes make you blind.

Your valuable energy will lose,

It quickly lessens your mental boost.

It is like a dose of poison for your health,

Always melt.

It is a dangerous temper,

All are badly hamper.

It leads your life into to the path of hell,

So, don't dig your own death of the well.

Before, it is going to block,

And give you a heavy dock.

Try to find out its real cause

So that you can pause.

Anger leads your life into to the path of hell,

So, don't dig your own death of the well.

﹏***﹏

23. Jealousy

Why you allow this growing weed?

Don't sow its dispersing seed.

If others are in adorable cloth,

Why you ought to spoil their worth?

If you don't know, how to admire!

You've no right to despair.

It is their fortune,

Why do you see their misfortune?

They are your peer,

You ought to cheer.

How do you feel?

When you dine the untidy meal,

It's like a poisoning pill,

Open its mouth to kill.

It makes your mind dirty,

And create tension in your unity.

Everything is earned by good deed,

It's the duty of all human creeds.

It sprouts the sin for another,

Fear from Godfather.

He loves all,

Because, you're His eternal soul.

When He closes His blessing eyes,

You ever revolve in this mortal dice.

So, fill your heart with pious,

And put-off this flame of jealous.

Don't sow the seed of jealousy in your mind.
It'll poison your mind, heart and soul.

〜***〜

24. Falsehood

When you make someone fool,

You feel cool.

But, it'll chase you

To catch you,

And it puts you into the jail,

Where is full of nails.

There is no shinning sun,

And you can't run.

It is the venom of the arrow,

Strike your heart in the barrow.

If you ever try to hide the truth,

You never get good fruit.

How long you'll keep enclose?

Someday it'll disclose.

It is a sin,

You must win!

You want to sell,

And spend your life in dreadful dale?

You know!

Yes or no.

The culprit of evil,

Is one-day reveal.

If you want to bind the mutual brotherhood,

Then, you must leave the habit of falsehood.

If you want to bind the mutual brotherhood,

Then, you must leave the habit of falsehood.

‿***‿

25. Insult

Whenever you'll get insulted,

Don't be disheartened, but wait for a big result.

If your fellow mates, make fun,

And trigger their laughing gun,

Even then, try to keep busy,

And try to move easily.

Control your opening mouth,

And stop your angry shout.

Work for goodwill,

Believe in your powerful will,

Don't take it as theirs cursing,

But, accept it as theirs blessing.

They are as your mentor,

Help you to become a good actor.

So, give as your examination,

Show them your determination.

Whenever you'll get insulted,

Don't be disheartened, but wait for a big result.

‿***‿

26. Relationship

It is as soft as cotton string,

Which ever need a strong ring?

When it'll break,

How it'll crack,

Nobody knows its secret shots,

So, bind it with a tight knot.

Once our mutual faith will lose,

We've to pay its heavy cost.

We'll suffocate all alone,

And we can't scream to call anyone.

Like no one could ever write anything on the beach of sand,

Because, it'll soon wash away from the tides' hand.

Stand together,

Sail further,

To the next shore,

We need our touching core.

But, if we divide ourselves,

We all drown in the sea depth.

Our bond is only tied with love,

But, not with the faded hope.

We could live in this world

When we learn how to hug all.

Our bond is only tied with love,

But, not with the faded hope.

∽***∽

27. Bad Memories

From your bad memories,

You'll only get the bag of worries.

It makes you cry,

And force you to die.

It'll turn your life haunted,

And you'll become faint hearted.

Everything will appear dark,

Everything will become your task.

So, stop your waves of flowing tears,

Don't be the victim of fears.

It'll block your success path,

And your doors of life will remain shut.

If you want to go beyond,

Then decide your own horizon.

Forget your dreadful past,

Nothing will long last.

When you'll learn to live again,

Then only you'll forget your pain.

From your bad memories,

You'll only get the bag of worries.

⁓***⁓

28. Face

If you've an ugly face,

It'll not the main cause.

But, your true heart,

And your right birth.

If anybody hates...!

Then, they will never be your genuine mate.

It's your sweet voice,

Make you the best choice.

If they will laugh at you,

And try to turn down your view.

Even, don't look down,

But try to be the great crown.

Always be sure,

And try to live in purity....

Be a wise!

Be a nice!

One day you'll see through your eyes,

These people will flock around you.

And when will you get your golden luck,

They will hug you.

It's your sweet voice,

Make you the best choice.

~***~

29. Smile

It's your melodious smile,

Spread from the mile.

It attracts very near,

And makes very dear.

It is like the blooming flower,

Splash the pleasant showers.

It is a song, which is sweet,

Ever ready to meet.

It is the fragrance of perfumes,

You feel the joy and the colors of fumes.

Your dusty journey of life becomes easy,

And brings you full of cozy.

It is your inner feelings which are visible in your eyes,

Where your hidden happiness lies.

You feel its chill,

And your faded life will dance with thrill.

It is your soft smile,

Not for a while.

It is your gifted jewel of nature,

Try to wear in your every juncture.

Your smile is like the blooming flower,

Splash the pleasant showers.

⌣***⌣

30. Shyness

Why do you feel shy?

If there is nothing to lie.

Ne'er hesitate to say,

Speak up whatever is laying.

Look at the glorious Sun's ray,

Nobody will dare to stop his ways.

If the Moon covers her elegance,

Then who will praise her glance!

The sweet flowers are soon dry-up,

Like the hopeless life is soon fed-up.

A fruit without taste

Is like the useless peels of waste.

If you hide your natural talent,

Then nobody will know yours intelligent.

It is your puzzling doubt,

Like the covering cloud.

Come out!

Take out!

Work for good,

And change your mood.

It is the act of silly,

You can't feed your hungry belly.

If you hide your natural talent,

Then nobody will know yours intelligent.

⌣***⌣

31. Meanings of Life

Look at the blue Sky!

It tells you to keep your goal high...

Look at the bright Sun!

It tells you to get up early and shine every day...

Look at the shinning Moon!

It tells you to remain cool and calm...

Look at the twinkling Stars!

They tell you to glow even in the darkness and to keep your hope...

Look at the flying Clouds!

It tells you to keep yourself free from all anxieties and worries....

Look at the mother Earth!

She tells you to keep your patience in every situation of your life....

Look at the Ocean!

It tells you to remain great and humble....

Look at the high peak mountains!

They tell you to stay firm and determine in your goals of life...

Look at the flowing rivers!

They tell you to keep doing your work continuously and persistently....

Look at the falling streams!

They tell you to maintain your coolness...

Look at the green trees!

They tell you to be kind and generous to every living being....

Look at the herd of animals!

It tells you to live in peace and unity...

Look at the flying birds!

They tell you to live in harmony...

Look at the blooming flowers!

They tell you to spread your love everywhere....

Look at the humming bees!

They tell you to remain active and labor without thinking about any result...

Look at the colorful butterflies!

They tell you to remain happy and high spirit...

Look around you!

Everything tells you the true meanings of your life.

There is a great meaning in everything....

﹏***﹏

32. The Right way

Follow the right way,

See the lighting ray,

Keep this as your target,

And whatever you did in the past, just forget.

Pace your move in forward,

Never see backward.

Learn to tackle the situation

With bold heart and action.

Do what is essential

With your potential.

Turn your life into a new shape,

Know its beauty and keep everything safe.

Pace your move in forward,

Never see backward.

Learn to tackle the situation with bold heart and action.

~***~

33. Light

Where there is light, there is life.

Where there is light, there is love.

Where there is light, there is peace.

Where there is light, there is happiness.

Where there is light, there is goodness.

Where there is light, there is blessing.

Where there is light, there is power.

Where there is light, there is energy.

Where there is light, there is knowledge.

Where there is light, there is wisdom.

Where there is light, there is divine.

Where there is light, there is serenity.

Where there is light, there is vision.

Where there is light, there is holiness.

Where there is light, there is salvation.

Where there is light, there is everything.

Where there is no light, there is only 'death'.

Where there is light, there is everything.

Where there is no light, there is only 'death'.

～***～

34. Your Nature

Your physical appearance

Is for a time being.

It'll perish with time.

Your infinite mind

Is a source of power.

It'll clean with divine thoughts.

Your beautiful heart

Is a core of love.

It'll fill with compassion.

Your twin eyes

Is not to wear the lens of proud,

It'll tire with age.

Your dimple cheek

Is not to wink.

It'll wrinkle with years.

Your pink lips

Is to smile sweetly.

It'll dry-up with the season.

Your delicious tongue

Is not to swing the sarcastic words.

It'll become tasteless with bitterness.

Your golden character

Is to polish the virtues.

It'll speak-up your true nature.

Your physical appearance

Is for a time being.

It'll perish with time.

‿***‿

35. Laziness

It is your laziness,

Corrodes and wither you.

You become like the useless metal.

It is your laziness,

Spread you dirt.

You become like the stagnant water.

It is your laziness,

Cover you with dust.

You become like barren soil.

It is your laziness,

Make you untidy.

You become like the dirty clothes.

It is your laziness,

Eat you blindly.

You become like the hollow tree.

It is your laziness,

Kill you slowly.

You become its prey.

‿***‿

36. An Idle Mind

Your life is beautiful.

Live with joy.

It'll become hell

If you make your mind idle.

Your life is beautiful.

Live with healthy and wealthy.

It'll become sick

If you make your mind idle.

Your life is beautiful.

Live with your great deeds.

It'll ruin

If you make your mind idle.

Your life is beautiful.

Live with your great ideas.

It'll become lifeless

If you make your mind idle.

Your life is beautiful.

Live with your great qualities.

It'll become meaningless

If you make your mind idle.

Your life is beautiful.

Live with your great ideas and actions.

It'll become lifeless if you make your mind idle.

᎔***᎔

37. Your Task!

If your task is to touch the sky,

You must overcome its limit.

If every time you're thrown,

You've to fly again.

If your task is to cross the ocean,

You must overcome its tides.

If every time you're drowned,

You've to swim again.

If your task is to climb the mountain,

You must overcome its height.

If every time you're fallen,

You've to get up again.

If your task is to win the battle,

You must overcome your weakness.

If every time you're defeated,

You've to fight back again.

If your task is to complete the race,

You must overcome a tougher opponent.

If every time you're beaten,

You've to run again.

If your task is to touch the sky,

You must overcome its limit.

〜***〜

38. The Greatness

The greatness of Earth

Lies in her life giving blessings.

The greatness of Sky

Lies in its vastness.

The greatness of Ocean

Lies in its deepness.

The greatness of Sun

Lies in its brightness.

The greatness of Moon

Lies in its dimness.

The greatness of River

Lies in its cleanliness.

The greatness of Trees

Lies in its greenery.

The greatness of Forest

Lies in its thickness.

The greatness of Flower

Lies in its fragrance.

The greatness of Fruit

Lies in its taste.

The greatness of Birds

Lies in their sweetness.

The greatness of Animals

Lies in their unity.

The greatness of Man

Lies in his righteous deeds.

87

The greatness of Man lies in his righteous deeds.

‿***‿

39. Give and Take

Your life is all about

Give and take.

If you give love,

In return, you'll get love.

Your life is all about

Give and take.

If you give hatred,

In return, you'll get hatred.

Your life is all about

Give and take.

If you give happiness,

In return, you'll get happiness.

Your life is all about

Give and take,

If you give a smile,

In return, you'll get a smile.

Your life is all about

Give and take.

If you give tears,

In return, you'll get tears.

Your life is all about

Give and take.

If you give blessing,

In return, you'll get the blessing.

Your life is all about

Give and take.

If you give the curse,

In return, you'll get cursed.

Your life is all about give and take.

90

⸾***⸾

40. Experiences of Life

We don't feel

The joy of laugh

If we never shed tears in life.

We don't feel

The gift of love

If we never give love in life.

We don't feel

The pains of others

If we never get hurt in life.

We don't feel

The heat of sun

If we never get wet in the rain.

We don't feel

The brightness of light

If we never spend in the darkness.

We don't feel

The current of water

If we never dive in the sea.

We don't feel

The taste of food

If we never get starve in life.

We don't feel

The sweetness of water

If we never get thirst in life.

We don't feel

The shivering of cold

If we never get sweat in life.

We don't feel

The softness of snow

If we never land on the dry sand.

We don't feel

The fragrance of flower

If we never get the smell of rotten.

We don't feel

The peace of loneliness

If we never spend in the crowd.

We don't feel

The excitement of success

If we never fail in life.

We don't feel

The beauties of life

If we never get the experiences of life.

*We don't feel the beauties of life if we never
get the experiences of life.*

∽***∽

41. Inner-Self

When you're lonely,

Who is speaking to you?

It's your inner-self,

It is your companion.

When you're lonely,

Who is guiding you?

It's your inner-self,

It is your conscience.

When you're lonely,

Who is hoping for you?

It's your inner-self,

It is your optimism.

When you're lonely,

Who is demoralizing you?

It's your inner-self,

It is your pessimism.

When you're lonely,

Who is fighting for you?

It's your inner-self,

It is your egoism.

When you're lonely,

Who is crying for you?

It's your inner-self,

It is your realization.

When you're lonely,

Who is laughing at you?

It's your inner-self,

It is your foolishness.

When you're lonely,

Who is disturbing you?

It's your inner-self,

It is your old memories.

When you're lonely,

Who is inspiring you?

It's your inner-self,

It is your faith.

When you're lonely,

Who is living with you?

It's your inner-self,

It is your thought.

When you're lonely,

Who is singing inside you?

It's your inner-self,

It is your love.

When you're lonely,

Who is dreaming for you?

It's your inner-self,

It is your expectation.

When you're lonely,

Who is playing with you?

It's your inner-self,

It's childish in you.

When you're lonely,

Who is sleeping with you?

It's your inner-self,

It is your peacefulness.

When you're lonely,

Who loves you?

It's your inner-self,

It is your core of heart.

When you're lonely,

Who is spying you?

It's your inner-self,

It guards you from the evils.

When you're lonely,

Who is with you?

It's your inner-self,

It is always with you.

Your inner-self is the best companion of your life.

⸙***⸙

42. Obstacles

It was the strong wind which attacked me.

I didn't see.

How those uncertain troubles came on my way?

I didn't get time to realize on that day.

I was blown away in the unknown place,

I couldn't replace.

I got a mighty blow.

It was very hard and made me very slow.

My days of life were tough,

I had no dare to rise up.

When I opened my dull eyes,

I saw the glowing sun, which turned into a big size.

He said something to me,

I heard his voice.

He asked me to stand and fight.

Then I found my self-belief,

I felt relief.

I re-discovered myself,

I dare to face the challenges without any help.

It was my great move,

It was the obstacles, which taught me how to tackle.

***It is only the obstacles of life that teach you
how to tackle in your life.***

∽***∽

43. Virtues

The Flower never tells its virtue.

But, its fragrance and sweetness

Attract the bees to come with it.

The Tree never tells its virtue.

But, its fruits and thick leaves

Attract the birds to make shelter in it.

The Forest never tells its virtue,

But, its evergreen and life giving boons

Attract the animals to dwell in it.

The River never tells its virtue.

But, its water resources

Attract the aquatic lives to live in it.

The Mountain never tells its virtue.

But, its steepness and great height

Attract the adventurous mind to climb in it.

The Ocean never tells its virtue.

But, its vastness and deepness

Attract the explorers to explore it.

The Great man never tells his virtue.

But, his great deeds

Attract the people to follow him.

The Great man never tells his virtue.

But, his great deeds attract the people to follow him.

⁓***⁓

44. Never Stop

The seasons are always changing.

They never stop.

The sun is always shinning.

It never stops.

The stars are always twinkling.

They never stop.

The wind is always blowing.

It never stops.

The river is always flowing.

It never stops.

The stream is always falling.

It never stops.

The trees are always growing.

They never stop.

The flowers are always blooming.

They never stop.

The birds are always flying.

They never stop.

The animals are always grazing.

They never stop.

The ants are always working.

They never stop.

These are the laws of nature,

They never stop.

Never stop in your life....

Always move ahead....

‿***‿

45. Your Questions!

What is this World?

This World is your battlefield.

Every day is a new battle for you.

Who are you?

You're the lone warrior.

Who are your enemies?

Your enemies are:

Lust,

Attachment,

Ego,

Greed,

And anger.

How could you face them?

You could face them with:

Patience,

Intellect,

Purity,

Compassion,

And love.

Who are challenging with you?

It's your own desires and attachments.

Who is your best friend?

It's your own conscience.

This World is your battlefield.

Every day is a new battle for you....

ᵔ***ᵔ

46. Ask yourself

When your heart is filled with hatred,

Then ask yourself- WHY?

Tell your heart to love.

When your heart is filled with jealousy,

Then ask yourself- WHY?

Tell your heart to be generous.

When your heart is filled with cruelties,

Then ask yourself- WHY?

Tell your heart to give mercy.

When your heart is filling with anger,

Then ask yourself- WHY?

Tell your heart to remain peaceful.

When your heart is filled with evils,

Then ask yourself- WHY?

Tell your heart to maintain divinity.

When your heart is filled with worry,

Then ask yourself- WHY?

Tell your heart to be merry.

When your heart is filled with negative,

Then ask yourself- WHY?

Tell your heart to be positive.

When your heart is filled with hatred,

Then ask yourself- WHY?

Tell your heart to love.

⌣***⌣

47. Parts of our Life

Life has two parts:

Birth and death;

Love and hatred;

Happiness and unhappiness;

Sweetness and bitterness;

Success and failure;

Day and night;

Brightness and darkness;

Company and lonely.

But, we've to live,

These are the parts our life.

Life has two parts:

Birth and death.

～***～

48. Failures

Failure is only a momentary,

It's a temporary.

No doubt, it will bend your road,

But it can't block your road.

Even success is not permanent,

You need your temperament.

Your hope is your golden ray,

Show you your hidden way.

Don't cry,

Never say die.

Believe yourself,

Work yourself.

Try to get up!

Try to rise up!

Don't make your heart weak,

Make your heart strong.

When you turn your failure into success,

Then you'll definitely get your success.

Never mind failure,

Your failure is the stepping-stone,

Which leads you to the ultimate milestone.

Failure is only a momentary,

It's a temporary.

No doubt, it will bend your road,

But it can't block your road.

⁀***⁀

49. The Best Way

It's always the best way

To change the direction of wind

If it is blowing violently towards you,

Rather than waiting to blow away.

It's always the best way

To change the route of water

If it is flowing turbulently towards you,

Rather than waiting to draw into.

It's always the best way

To change the path of smoking fire

If it is polluting the air towards you,

Rather than waiting to suffocate in it.

It's always the best way

To change the arising situation

If it is disturbing your life

Rather than waiting to die within.

It's always the best way

To change the arising situation

If it is disturbing your life

Rather than waiting to die within.

‿***‿

50. Today and Yesterday

Whoever you're today,

Whatever you're today,

Wherever you're today,

This is significant for you.

Whoever you were yesterday,

Whatever you were yesterday,

Wherever you were yesterday,

That is not significant for you.

Whatever you're thinking today,

Whatever you're working today,

Whatever you're getting today,

Wherever you're going today,

This is significant for you.

Whatever you were thinking yesterday,

Whatever you were working yesterday,

Whatever you were getting yesterday,

Wherever you were going yesterday,

That is not significant for you.

Everything depends upon today.

Nothing depends upon yesterday.

So, forget yesterday

And work today.

Everything depends upon today.

Nothing depends upon yesterday.

⸰***⸰

51. If You Are......

If you're a thinker,

And if you can!

Give the meanings of life

To the dying mind.

If you're a philosopher,

And if you can!

Advice the importance of life

To the dying soul.

If you're a writer,

And if you can!

Write the experiences of life

To the dying life.

If you're a teacher,

And if you can!

Teach the lessons of life

To the dying heart.

If you're an explorer,

And if you can!

Inspire the adventures of life

To the dying nerve.

If you're an inventor,

And if you can!

Present the fascinations of life

To the dying hands.

If you're a discoverer,

And if you can!

Visualize the mysteries of life

To the dying eyes.

If you're a healer,

And if you can!

Bless the pleasures of life

To the dying health.

If you're a builder,

And if you can!

Build the treasures of life

To the dying head.

If you're a musician,

And if you can!

Compose the music of life

To the dying voice.

If you're a singer,

And if you can!

Sing the songs of life

To the dying love.

If you're an artist,

And if you can!

Paint the colors of life

To the dying man.

If you're a simple man,

And if you can!

Mould your simple life

To live a happy life.

‿***‿

52. Silent Sleep

Don't resign so early

From this life.

Never say good-bye.

You've to do many things

For yourself and for your beloved ones.

If you want to earn,

You must learn.

If you want to receive something,

Then first, you've to give something.

Lead yourself; lead everyone.

Do your own deeds.

Live your life for a noble cause,

And serve the life of the needy.

Guide your footprint

To the world before you going to silent sleep.

Don't resign so early

From this life.

Never say good-bye.

You've to do many things

For yourself and for your beloved ones.

ᘏ***ᘏ

53. Except You!

In this world, no one is yours,

All are own self.

Everything is your own.

Who is yours?

Who are others?

You can't say.

Who are your friends?

Who are your enemies?

You can't deny.

The warning bell tells you

The tales of smiling and weeping.

Your life is not run by anybody,

But, with yourself.

There is no one,

Only except you.

Your life is not run by anybody,

But, with yourself.

There is no one,

Only except you.

⁓***⁓

54. Disguise

We're wearing an ordinary dress.

Everything is in His (Almighty God) hands.

Whether man or woman,

Whether birds or animals,

Everything is His creations.

We all are living beings

Living for a time being.

Try to become like a sage,

But never try to become like a savage.

Try to pass your loving kiss,

But never try to pass your poisonous hiss.

Leave your natures of cat,

Leave the life of a rat.

Your life is not to sting,

But to live the life of the king.

Life is full of hard task,

Wear out your devil's mask.

Don't live in disguise,

Come out from your dark cell.

Live the life of nobility,

And try to become the crown of global.

Life is full of hard task,

Wear out your devil's mask.

Don't live in disguise,

Come out from your dark cell.

⁓***⁓

55. Your Fight

You've to fight for good cause,

But, not for vice.

You've to fight for right,

But, not for wrong deeds.

You've to fight with love,

But, not with hatred.

You've to fight with divinity,

But' not with evil.

You've to fight with your egos,

But, not with your life.

You've to fight with yourself,

But, not with others.

You're the lone soldier in your fight,

So, fight with your full might.

You're the lone soldier in your fight,

So, fight with your full might.

‿***‿

56. Your Thoughts

If your thoughts are strong,

You feel strong.

If your thoughts are weak,

You feel weak and sick.

If your thoughts are positive,

You feel positive.

If your thoughts are negative,

You feel negative.

If your thoughts are good,

You feel good.

If your thoughts are bad,

You feel bad.

If your thoughts are right,

You feel right.

If your thoughts are wrong,

You feel guilty.

If your thoughts are great,

You feel great.

If your thoughts are small,

You feel small and timid.

Everything is all about your thoughts.

You're ruled by own thoughts.

Everything is all about your thoughts.

You're ruled by own thoughts.

∼***∼

57. Think!

If there is no sun in the sky,

Think!

What will happen?

There will be only darkness everywhere.

If there is no Moon in the sky,

Think!

What will happen?

The sky will become ugly.

If there are no stars in the sky,

Think!

What will happen?

The sky will become empty.

If there is no Earth,

Think!

What will happen?

There will be no life.

If there is no air,

Think!

What will happen?

We'll die.

If there are no clouds,

Think!

What will happen?

There will be no rain.

If there is no water,

Think!

What will happen?

There will be no creation.

If there is no tree,

Think!

What will happen?

There will be no greenery.

If there is no flower,

Think!

What will happen?

There will be no fragrance.

If there are no birds,

Think!

What will happen?

There will be no songs.

If there is no man,

Think!

What will happen?

There will be no civilization.

If we've no house,

Think!

What will happen?

We'll become a nomad.

If there is no wisdom,

Think!

What will happen?

We'll become like animals.

If there is no love,

Think!

What will happen?

We'll become like the devil.

If we've no friends,

Think!

What will happen?

We'll become lonely.

If there is nothing in this world,

Think!

What will happen?

Everything will become meaningless.

If there is no love,

Think!

What will happen?

We'll become like the devil.

*ⸯ***ⸯ*

58. *Love*

Love yourself,

Love your mother,

Love your father,

Love your brother,

Love your sister,

Love your spouse,

Love your friends,

Love your relatives,

Even love your enemies,

And love every creature of this world.

If you know how to love,

Then you know the art of living.

Love teaches you everything,

Without love, there is nothing.

Love is the mother of everything,

Live your life with love.

If you know how to love,

Then you know the art of living.

⌒***⌒

59. *Keep Busy!*

The Sun is always shinning,

He has full of rays,

Because he is busy.

The Wind is always blowing,

She has full of power,

Because she is busy.

The River is always flowing,

It has full of resources,

Because it is busy.

The Trees are always growing,

They have full of life,

Because they are busy.

The Flowers are always blooming,

They have full of colors,

Because they are busy.

The Ants are always moving,

They have full of stamina,

Because they are busy.

The Bees are always flying,

They have full of sweets,

Because they are busy.

If you're busy in your work,

Then, you'll always progress in your life.

**Always remember that the busiest man is
the happiest man in this world.**

‿***‿

60. The Blowing Air

If I was be the blowing wind,

I'll fly everywhere.

I'll try to clean the dirty mind.

I'll try to blow away all the stresses of mind.

I'll try to give fresh air.

I'll try to give lights of fairness.

I'll try to wash away all the worries.

I'll try to give the blessing of merry.

I'll try to give the everlasting peace.

I'll try to give all bliss.

I'll try to give the healing touch.

I'll try to make all pure.

I'll try to give my heartiest wishes.

I'll try to give my loving kisses.

I'll try to spread the messages of love.

I'll try to sprout the blooming hope.

Try to spread the messages of love far and wide and make this world a better place.

‿***‿

61. Why Not You!

If the Sun loves to rise,

Then, why not you?

Learn to rise....

If the Moon loves to shine,

Then, why not you?

Learn to shine....

If the Stars loves to twinkle,

Then, why not you?

Learn to twinkle with your smile....

If the Clouds love to shed rain,

Then, why not you?

Learn to shed the rain of joy and happiness.....

If the Wind loves to blow,

Then, why not you?

Learn to blow away your negative thoughts and energies.....

If the River love to flow,

Then, why not you?

Learn to flow towards your destiny....

If the Trees love to grow,

Then, why not you?

Learn to grow and progress....

If the Trees love to grow,

Then, why not you?

Learn to grow and progress....

〜***〜

62. Born and Die

Life is like a flower,

Sometime it gets the drops of the shower.

Sometime faded with changing seasons.

Sometime blooming with new season.

It spreads her fragrance,

It attracts with her elegance.

Sometime the happiness of butterflies hovers around her,

Sometime the sucking bees surround her.

But, with the setting of sun,

Everything will run.

And she will get down,

To sleep forever on the ground.

It's the cycle of nature,

Born and die are its feature.

Life is like a flower,

Sometime it gets the drops of the shower.

Sometime faded with changing seasons.

Sometime blooming with new season.

༄***༄

63. People

There are many people,

Some are looking very simple,

Some are appearing very complex.

They have different perplex.

But, whoever you meet,

Try to greet.

Some may behave friendly,

Some may show their envy.

Not all are equal and same,

But, you don't need to feel shame.

You just pass your goodwill

Without committing ill.

Our life is too short,

Don't make your blood hot.

Try to live in every moment

With your great movement.

Our life is too short,

Don't make your blood hot.

Try to live in every moment

With your great movement.

⌒***⌒

64. Silent !

Look at the sun!

How silently...

It is glowing.

Look at the Moon!

How silently...

It is shinning.

Look at the Stars!

How silently...

They are twinkling.

Look at the water!

How silently...

It is flowing.

Look at the air!

How silently..........

It is blowing.

Look at the trees!

How silently………

They are growing.

Look at the flowers!

How silently……….

They are blooming.

Look at the animals!

How silently……….

They are moving.

Look at the birds!

How silently………

They are flying.

Look at yourself!

How are you?

Are you silent... ?

There is only one way to live...

That is the way to live silent.

There is only one way to live...

That is the way to live silent.

ᔐ***ᔐ

65. Take Sometime

Take some time to think,

Take some time to look,

Take some time to talk,

Take some time to walk,

Take some time to work,

Take some time to know yourself.

Let's allow the whole cosmos comes to you.

Feel the thrills of the whole universe.

Take some time to yourself.

Take some time to know yourself.

Let's allow the whole cosmos comes to you.

⌒***⌒

66. Yourself

Think yourself,

Act yourself,

Look yourself,

Watch yourself,

Teach yourself,

Learn yourself,

Read yourself,

Recite yourself,

Compose yourself,

Sing yourself,

Work yourself,

Sail yourself,

Discover yourself,

Explore yourself,

Experiment yourself,

Find yourself,

Know yourself,

When you know yourself,

Then, you find your true self.

When you know yourself,

Then, you find your true self.

〜***〜

67. The Blooming Flower

The blooming flower looks very beautiful,

It is silent and serene.

It is innocent as a little child.

It smiles every time,

Whether hot or cold;

Whether rainy or sunny.

In every season,

It keeps her lovely smiling,

Whether it is growing in the garden;

Or it is growing in the roadside;

Whether it is growing in the courtyard;

Or it is growing in the backyard,

It never lost its magical charm.

Every time it spreads her fragrance.

It attracts everybody's eyes.

The tiny bees; the colorful butterflies, and the small humming birds

Are flying nearby.

They love her sweet honey.

Its fantastic color changes our moods.

We feel joy and pleasures.

Even it melts the heart of a stone-hearted man.

It steals the heart of every man.

It tells us the wisdom of nature.

It teaches us the lessons of love, compassion, purity, and kindness.

It is how nice if the fragrance of the flower is in the heart of every man.

And every time it blooms in everybody's face.

It is how nice if the fragrance of the flower is in the heart of every man.

And every time it blooms in everybody's face.

⸮***⸮

68. I Thank You!

I Thank You!

O! My dear Life.

Because,...............

You taught me the sweet taste of love.

You taught me the bitter taste of hatred.

You taught me the bonds of friendship.

You taught me the bondage of foes.

You taught me the joys of happiness.

You taught me the agony of sorrows.

You taught me the feelings of loneliness.

You taught me the intimacy of a good companionship.

You taught me the godliness of divinity.

You taught me the evil devils.

You taught me the journey to 'Death'.

You taught me the lessons to 'Alive'.

You taught me the true meanings of 'Life'.

You taught me the secrets of this 'Life'.

I Thank You!

O! My dear Life.

Life is a great teacher.

It teaches you a great lesson....

⁓***⁓

69. You Can See………

In the rays of Sun,

You can see its energy.

In the lights of Moon,

You can see its calmness.

In the twinkling Stars,

You can see their friendliness.

In the standing Mountain,

You can see its strength.

In the flying Clouds,

You can see their gentleness.

In the waves of Sea,

You can see their continuity.

In the falling Stream,

You can see its persistence.

In the flowing River,

You can see its smoothness.

In the leaves of Tree,

You can see their patience.

In the drops of dew,

You can see their purities.

In the songs of Birds,

You can see their devotions.

In the humming of Bees,

You can see their freedom.

In the blooming of Flowers,

You can see their smiles.

In the flying Butterflies,

You can see their happiness.

In the walking of Ants,

You can see their unity.

In Your life,

You can see love everywhere.

Open your inner-eyes to see the beauty of this world...

ᔛ***ᔛ

70. Love Yourself!

Nothing can make you fly,

But, love.

Nothing can make you joy.

But, love,

Nothing can make you sad,

But, love.

Nothing can make you smile,

But, love.

Nothing can make you cry,

But, love.

Nothing can make you mad,

But, love.

Nothing can make you sing,

But, love.

Nothing can make you dance,

But, love.

Nothing can make you die,

But, love.

Nothing can make you alive.

But, love.

Nothing can make you complete,

But, love.

Nothing can make you feel wonderful,

But, love.

Nothing can make you live.

But, love.

Nothing can make you love,

But, love itself.

Nothing can make you live.

But, love.

Nothing can make you love,

But, love itself.

‿***‿

71. You're the Master of Your Own

You're the creator of your own,

You can create anything.

You're the maker of your own,

You can do anything.

You're the discoverer of your own,

You can discover anything.

You're the inventor of your own,

You can invent anything.

Whether for your life or your world,

Whether for your nature or your future.

Believe in yourself.

You can!

Nothing is impossible for you,

Everything is possible for you.

You're the maker of your own,

You're the master of your own.

Believe in yourself.

You can!

Nothing is impossible for you,

Everything is possible for you.

You're the maker of your own,

You're the master of your own.

﹏***﹏

72. You are born to be Wise!

You're not born to be bad,

But, you're born to be good.

You're not born to be weak,

But, you're born to be strong.

You're not born to be poor,

But, you're born to be rich.

You're not born to be small,

But, you're born to be great.

You're not born to be low,

But, you're born to be high.

You're not born to fall,

But, you're born to rise.

You're not born to be slow,

But, you're born to be fast.

You're not born to hate,

But, you're born to love.

You're not born to be sad,

But, you're born to be happy.

You're not born to be impatience,

But, you're born to be patience.

You're not born to be pessimistic,

But, you're born to be optimistic.

You're not born to be a failure,

But, you're born to be a winner.

You're not born to be a foe,

But, you're born to be friends.

You're not born to be sinner,

But, you're born to be pious.

You're not born to be ignorant,

But, you're born to be wise.

You're not born to be a failure,

But, you're born to be a winner.

༄***༄

73. You've to live Your Life

Life is a shadow,

Sometime it's dark.

Sometime it's glow.

When the lights fall on it,

It shows its reflecting heat.

It shines as the rising sun,

And help you to run.

But, at the same time,

It gives you both tears and smiles.

The shadow formed in your front and in your back.

In the morning, it's long,

In the evening, it's long;

At noon, it's short,

But, you've to keep your life's cord.

If one side of your life is bright,

The other side of your life will be night.

Happiness and sorrow both are walking together,

You can't hold them any longer.

If the former gives, you delight,

The later gives you a fright.

It's the part of your life,

But, anyhow you've to live your life.

Happiness and sorrow both are walking together,

You can't hold them any longer.

If the former gives, you delight,

The later gives you a fright.

It's the part of your life,

But, anyhow you've to live your life.

‿***‿

74. You're born as the Brave Soldier

You're born as the brave soldier,

You've to walk with the tall shoulder.

Your foremost duty is to fight,

It's your right.

You've to go day and night,

It's your pride.

You've to reach far and wide,

With your own solely might.

You've a strong weapon,

Go on and on.

Clear your foggy eyesight,

Search your lost light.

Every time you'll face the deadliest defeat,

But, you've to grip your slipping feet.

If you can, hug your death, which is your greatest fate.

But, never lay down,

Even you break down.

Never give up!

Raise your thumps up!

If you die for your motherland,

She will surely reward you with her blessing garland.

You're born as the brave soldier,

You've to walk with the tall shoulder.

Your foremost duty is to fight,

It's your right.

‿***‿

75. Love is a Prayer

Love is a prayer,

It's enriching when we share.

Love is a divine worship,

It mends the bond of friendship.

Love is devotion,

That changes one's life notion.

Love is pious,

It binds us.

Love is the only medicine,

That cures all our sins.

Love is the language of our heart,

That brings our heart to heart.

Nobody can live without it,

Love is the greatest feat.

Love cools down the fire of hatred,

And bring us the rain of sacred.

Love clears our heart and soul,

And build our house in the blissful world.

173

Love is a divine worship,

It mends the bond of friendship.

‿***‿

76. The Law of Natural Ordination

Everything is running by its rotation,

It's the law of natural ordination.

If you've a gala day,

Who knows tomorrow you've a cumbersome day.

If you misuse your power,

Soon you'll blow away like the ash power.

Everybody has own right,

Never hurt anybody.

Give your heart's regard,

Act as their best ward.

Whether giant or wee,

Whether he or she,

If you ever try to dominate,

Soon you'll eliminate.

Never try to roam like the insane elephant,

Else, you'll meet your the end.

A day will come when you'll fall down,

And no one will come to rescue your crown.

Never try to roam like the insane elephant,

Else, you'll meet your the end.

A day will come when you'll fall down,

And no one will come to rescue your crown.

‿***‿

77. You will never regain it!

Where are you standing right now?

How are you posing right now?

Look at yourself,

See your footsteps,

See your moving feet,

Change your outfit.

Look all around,

The world is not round,

It's becoming flat,

So, don't be late.

Now the world is becoming too small,

Everything comes too close,

And nothing remains old.

Peel out your sophisticated costumes,

Feel the new fume.

But, one thing!

Never forget your true self,

Your identity,

Your dignity,

Once you lost it,

You'll never regain it.

Never forget your true self,

Your identity,

Your dignity,

Once you lost it,

You'll never regain it.

‿***‿

78. In search of life

In search of life,

I'm wandering hither and thither.

Sometime here,

Sometime there,

Whether I'd get my shinning dream,

Or I'd get mirage of the beam.

I don't know.

But I was on my way.

On the curving road of life,

I'm walking all alone, even biting a sharp knife.

Every moment I'm facing tests.

But I try my best.

Whether I'd get success or failure.

I don't know,

But I was on my way.

Into the cave of darkness,

I'm trying to get some brightness.

Sometime I'm getting a hard knock,

Sometime I'm getting harsh shock.

But I was on my way.

Every moment if you face hard test,

Give your best,

Whether you'd get success or failure.

Don't worry!

Move ahead on your own way.

‿***‿

79. Under Your Feet

Let the whole world laugh at you,

But never leave your self-worth.

It's their reason,

But, never put-off your vision.

Maintain your own dignity,

Create your identity.

Keep your self-esteem.

Like the boiling steam.

Never beg for anything,

You're not born to sting.

But, you're here to rule,

Never become a fool.

Go on with one mind,

Follow your own lifeline.

You've a mighty heart,

You're only here to make a new art.

Just you need to re-discover yourself,

To find out your lost shelf.

Then everything will be under your feet,

You'll reach in the highest summit.

Let the whole world laugh at you,

But never leave your self-worth.

⁓***⁓

80. You're a Great Soul

If you've an ink and a pen,

Then you've everything in your hand.

Just jot down!

But never break down.

It's your powerful weapon,

Don't beg with an empty spoon.

You're very special,

You're not alone.

Don't worry!

Always be merry!

Life is not a blank page,

Turn it as a golden age.

You've rights to write your own story,

You've rights to make a new history.

Create your own book

To reveal your outlook.

Tell the world

That you're a great soul.

You're bound to get your destiny.

Create your own book

To reveal your outlook.

Tell the world

That you're a great soul.

᠊***᠊

81. Rub your tears

Rub your tears,

Forget your fears.

These are the sign of your weakness.

These bring you unhappiness.

Forget your dreadful past,

Else, it'll be overcast.

You're here to become an outclass,

You belong to a special class.

If you run away like an outlaw,

You'll get a very hard blow.

You're not a coward,

You're here for your reward.

Don't do anything in a hurry,

It'll bring you worry.

Be calm and patient,

Your Lord will bless you the grand present.

Don't make the house of glass,

Make it for long lasting.

You're in your creation,

You're in own destruction.

Everything is in your reach,

Just you need to become rich.

Go ahead...............

Don't be sad.

You're bound to get your destiny,

Even you're very tiny.

⌣***⌣

82. You're very special

You've to open your closed door,

Even you're very poor.

If there is a doubt,

Even you've to go out.

You've to go............

Even you'll face woe.

How your life will turn round,

When you'll get your rising dawn.

You can't say.

After every dark night,

You'll get the rising sunlight.

Everybody is born for something,

Don't feel that you're nothing.

Don't pause,

Your life is for a good cause.

Life is to live,

But, not to die.

Find out your strong point,

To know your turning point.

Don't spend your life in dreadful cell,

Because you're very special.

After every dark night,

You'll get the rising sunlight.

~***~

83. The Smiling Lady

Success never comes early,

You've to work daily.

Worship in your soil,

Even shed your sweats,

But keep your handy toil.

Anchor your aim,

Your labor never makes you lame.

Every day is your new test,

You're not born to take a rest.

Don't afraid of the burning sun,

If you want your lively fun.

It's not easy,

It's not for lazy.

It takes time,

But it'll mould you fine.

She wears her disguise dress in shady,

It's too difficult to please the smiling lady.

But she'll definitely smile you one day.

Every day is your new test,

You're not born to take a rest.

⌣***⌣

84. For Your Next Mission

O! Crying eyes,

O! Dying hearts,

O! Tiring minds,

O! Sleeping souls,

Love your life,

Love your world,

You're the most lovable,

You're the most valuable,

Don't waste your beautiful life!

Life is all about hardship,

Life is all about worship.

Why are you fooled by the self-created illusion?

Why you indulged in the bad dilution?

Come out!

Get out!

Stand up!

Wake up!

Do something for yourself,

Do something for all.

Be steady!

Get ready!

For your next mission.

You're the most valuable,

Don't waste your beautiful life!

Life is all about hardship,

Life is all about worship.

◡***◡

85. The Little Candle

In the dark night,

When there is no sight,

The little candle is burning alone,

Fighting all alone.

Without fear,

Without care,

Fighting with the wild wind,

Fighting with the mad black queen.

With a thin wick,

Without feeling sick.

She doesn't know any scream,

She only knows her beam.

She sacrifices her life,

For the happiness of others' life.

She keeps her vows,

Even she keeps away her woes.

She doesn't know any curse,

But, she tells us to search,

The path of light,

And to feel the delight.

Don't forget to fight even you are alone in your life...

﹏***﹏

86. Never Forget

Your life is not like an empty bucket,

Never fall in the dirty racket.

Fill it with great thoughts,

Don't drop the chain of blocks.

Don't grow the weeds of greed,

It'll cover your clean deed.

Before, you would see the shining sun in the sky blue,

Cultivate the moral value.

Never allow the sewages to stagnate in your brain,

Sweep your foul smelling drain.

Turn your two hands as the hard steel,

So that in your green field you could till.

Don't allow your iron rode to corrode,

Decide your leading route.

You're not born to get rust,

But, you're born to shine.

Wash away!

Blow away!

You've right to have your gold,

Never forget your life's goal.

You're not born to get rust,

But, you're born to shine.

〜***〜

87. Mirror

Life is like a mirror,

Sometimes it shows you horror.

Sometimes it shows you good look.

But, sometimes it becomes faded with fog.

When you talk with it,

When you smile with it,

It smiles back,

Because, it acts you to act.

You see, left as right,

You see right as left.

But, it tells you the truth,

Which you actually suite.

You've many different faces,

That binds you with hard laces.

Find out your true self,

And try to come out from the dark shelf.

It reflects your true-identity,

So, maintain your own dignity.

Find out your true self,

And try to come out from the dark shelf.

∽***∽

88. Don't Sit Down

Don't sit down,

Don't look down,

Stand up!

Look up!

Keep your aim high,

Try to fly high.

Go ahead in your destiny

With single minded,

Don't divert your mind.

Concentrate on your work.

Don't measure your work with its size.

Because every work has its own importance,

Don't think about its result,

But do your work.

Whatever you want to do,

Do right now.

Never postpone anything.

Never forget that 'work is worship'

Then only you'll get success in your life.

Don't measure your work with its size.

Because every work has its own importance,

Don't think about its result,

But do your work.

～***～

89. Love is Music

Love is music,

It composes in the core of our heart.

It's sweet,

It's awesome.

Every moment it sings in our heart.

It's silently flowing in our heart,

Its softness touches our heart,

Its songs make us divine,

Its melody makes our life pious,

Its every node fills our heart with bliss,

Its every rhythm gives us the meanings of life,

Love is the universal song,

That sings in everybody's hearts.

With its music no one can live in this universe,

Because love is eternal,

Because love is our integral part of our life,

Without its music, our life is quiet.

It's only the music of love that makes our life meaningful.

Because love is our integral part of our life,

Without its music, our life is quiet.

⸜***⸝

90. The Flying Feather

Life is like the flying feather,

Sometime here,

Sometime there.

When it leaves the mother's body,

It doesn't remain anymore for anybody.

Wherever the wind blows,

It freely dances to flow.

It has lovely fur,

That swing in the air.

Where it travels,

It doesn't know its dwell.

It is soft and light,

But, its desire is to see the rays of light.

It is tiny,

It has no destiny.

It only flies,

But, sometimes it silently lies.

Sometimes it falls down,

And sometimes it sleeps on the ground.

Life is like the flying feather,

Sometime here,

Sometime there.

‿***‿

91. Wait for the Right Season

Before summer season,

There will be no heating of Sun.

Before Windy season,

There will be no blowing of stormy wind.

Before spring season,

There will be no blooming of flowers.

Before winter season,

There will be no falling of dew and ice.

Before Rainy season,

There will be no pattering of rainfall.

Before autumn season,

There will be no shedding of leaves.

Before any season,

There will be no season of anything.

Before time,

There will be nothing in our life.

Wait for the right season

To celebrate for special reasons,

With cool and calm,

Without losing your heart.

Then, one day you'll see the right season will knock at your door step.

Before time,

There will be nothing in our life.

Wait for the right season.

᷈***᷈

92. Hunger

It is the hunger,

Makes the man to go.....

It is the hunger,

Makes the man to run........

It is the hunger,

Makes the man to chase........

It is the hunger,

Makes the man to challenge..........

It is the hunger,

Makes the man to fight........

It is the hunger,

Makes the man to grab.........

It is the hunger,

Makes the man to steal........

It is the hunger,

Makes the man to beg........

It is the hunger,

Makes the man to sell.........

It is the hunger,

Makes the man to work........

It is the hunger,

Makes the man to labor........

It is the hunger,

Makes the man to pray........

If there is no hunger,

There will be nothing in this world....

Your hunger is the reason of everything.....

Either good or bad!

Your hunger is the reason of everything.....

Either good or bad!

⤳***⤳

93. Like a Bicycle

Life is like the bicycle,

Its world is moving in the path of the cycle.

It has two wheels,

That is revolving by the order of Heaven's will.

The human soul is merely a rider,

He has to go further.

So, he must know how to balance it,

Then he can ride it.

Because, as he moves its pedals,

It moves on and on....

But as he stops it,

He'll fall down.

With his applying force it runs,

And every spoke spins with fun.

It is made to ride,

It is not made to keep aside.

Our life is to live,

Our life is to view the greatest site,

But not to die.

The human soul is merely a rider,

He has to go further.

〜***〜

94. Like an Egg

Life is like an egg,

It's very delicate.

Even it covered with a hard shell,

Once it'll fall down from your hand,

It'll lose its life's worth.

It'll break.

You only get its broken pieces,

Handle it with your loving heart,

Hold it with your caring hands.

Hatch it like the mother hen,

She cares her loving dear.

She sticks to herself day and night,

Even she forgets her delight.

After devoting her test of patience,

One day her young ones come out,

And she feels proud.

Life is like an egg,

It's very delicate.

Even it covered with a hard shell,

Once it'll fall down from your hand,

It'll lose its life's worth.

◟***◞

95. Agony of Life

It's the burning of the flame,

Which has burnt my name.

I died before my death,

It's the tragedy of my fate.

Everywhere only the flashing of ashes,

I couldn't blink my eyes.

I need a little drop of water,

To put-off this terrible, shatter.

My heart is breaking like a piece of glasses,

No one is with me to stop my lonely clashes.

My beloved peers are in their fast asleep,

None of them is awake to peep.

My dream house burnt,

And I'm getting hurt.

My blood and flesh swelled,

And I'm bound to leave my dwell.

I've no more shelter,

My life is flying hither and thither.

Now, O my Lord!

Hold me in your blessing cord.

Save me from this dreadful agony,

And show me the life giving new destiny.

Now, O my Lord!

Hold me in your blessing cord.

Save me from this dreadful agony,

And show me the life giving new destiny.

〜***〜

96. A Blooming Flower

In every season,

It blooms with its colorful looks.

In hot summer season,

It resists the burning heat of Sun.

In cold winter season,

It resists the freezing cold ice.

In dry autumn season,

It resists the welting of the dry season.

In blooming spring season,

It gets the beauty of nature.

In rainy season,

It feels the falling of heavy rainfall.

In windy season,

It feels the dusty blowing of wind.

In every season,

It never cries,

Even in dry.

It ever keeps its smiling face.

Wherever it blooms,

Everywhere it passes for a gentle smile.

Everywhere it diffuses its sweet fragrance.

Everywhere it attracts with its beautiful colors.

Everywhere it spreads its happiness.

In every season,

It ever appears attractive,

It ever keeps its beauty,

It ever maintains its purity.

It is a blooming beautiful flower,

Inspires us to live in peace,

Its every single petal gives us a smile of gentle kiss,

And ask us not to miss the joy of life,

No matter how many harsh seasons knock in our life.

Its every single petal gives us a smile of gentle kiss,

And ask us not to miss the joy of life,

*No matter how many harsh seasons knock
in our life.*

⸢***⸥

97. Life is action and reaction

Life is all about action and reaction,

When you give positive action,

In return, you'll get its positive reaction.

As much as you apply, force on anything,

As much as it reflects its force on you.

In the walk of life, you can't take breaks,

Because life is not a walkie-talkie movie that you can retake.

Whatever life will play with you,

You can't replay.

It'll never be back flowing,

Because life is like a flowing river that ever flowing on its own natural flow.

As you treat with your life,

As it treats with you.

As you never deny that good deeds always give good results,

And bad deeds always give bad results.

Like a flowering plant always bears a beautiful flower,

Like a thorny plant always, bear spine like thorns.

What do you want in your life?

It depends on you.

If you're in the search of a gold mine,

You'll get its shinning gold.

If you're in search of coal mine,

You'll get its blackish coal.

In your life every small step will count,

No matter where you want to mount.

Your one right step will lead you at the doorstep of heaven.

Your one wrong step will lead you at the doorstep of hell.

Before anything going worse on your life's track,

Turn back your heading steps from its crack.

So that you can move forward,

Leaving behind your unnoticed footmark.

What do you want in your life?

It depends on you.

If you're in the search of a gold mine,

You'll get its shinning gold.

If you're in search of coal mine,

You'll get its blackish coal.

‿***‿

98. Good Things will come to you

When you see good things,

When you think good thoughts,

When you say good words,

When you do good works,

When you meet good people,

When you act good actions,

When you cultivate good habits,

When you earn good hobbies,

Then good things will embrace you forever.

You'll never deviate yourself from good things.

It'll always hold you from bad things.

So, keep it in your life forever.

When you become good,

Everyone will be yours.

When you become good,

Everything will be yours.

When you become good,

Your life will become good.

When you become good,

Your world will become good.

Always remember that good things always follow good things,

And bad things always follow bad things.

Always remember that good things always follow good things,

And bad things always follow bad things.

⁓***⁓

99. Change Yourself

If you ever want to read something,

Then read a book of life.

It'll teach you the wisdom of life.

If you ever want to learn something,

Then learn the art of life,

It'll adorn your life.

If you ever want to say something,

Then say a word of goodwill,

It'll tell give you the blessings of life.

If you ever want to listen to something,

Then listen to a voice of your conscience,

It'll introduce you with the truth of life.

If you ever want to look something,

Then look a life of a great man,

It'll show you the real worth of life.

If you ever want to give something,

Then give a word of love,

It'll return you a romance of life.

If you ever want to accept something,

Then accept a word of blessings,

It'll bring you bliss of life.

If you ever want to get-rid of from something,

Then get-rid of from your bad deeds,

It'll purify your life.

If you ever want to do something,

Then do a great work,

It'll bring you a great contentment in your life.

If you ever want to change something,

Then change yourself,

It'll make you a complete man in your life.

If you ever want to change something,

Then change yourself,

It'll make you a complete man in your life.

⌇***⌇

100. Grow Your Life Everyday

As a small plant grows every day,

To become a big tree one day.

Grow your life every day,

To become a complete man.

Grow your thoughts every day,

To be happy in your life.

Grow your knowledge every day,

To be knowledgeable in your life.

Grow your wisdom every day,

To be wise in your life.

Grow your intellect every day,

To judge yourself in your life.

Grow your work every day,

To do great deeds in your life.

Grow your life every day,

To live your life in prosperity.

Grow your world every day,

To spend your life in peace.

226

Grow your life every day to become a complete man.

﹏***﹏

About the author:

Birister Sharma is a full time author. He is also an avid reader. He loves reading, writing, and motivation. He has penned down dozens of self-help motivational books and novels so far.

You may contact him @ birister2007@gmail.com